Theater & Dance Photographs

FRANCIS LEDERER, Berlin, 1929.

Lotte Jacobi

Theater & Dance Photographs

Introduction by Cornell Capa

Countryman Press ■ Woodstock, Vermont

Design and production by Guy Russell
Text and picture editing by A. Ambats
Typeset by Williams Graphic Service
Printed at Acme Printing
Bound at the New Hampshire Bindery

93864

Library of Congress Cataloging in Publication Data

Jacobi, Lotte, 1896–
  Theatre and dance photographs.

  1. Actors—Europe—Portraits.   2. Dancers—
Europe—Portraits.   I. Title.
PN2570.J3 1982   792′.028′0922 [B]   82-14514
ISBN 0-914378-93-7 (pbk.)

INTRODUCTION

Lotte Jacobi is a contemporary miracle. Her longevity and vigor of mind, her faithfulness to old-fashioned virtues, her never-dated quality of taste and work, are all marks of her remarkable uniqueness.

Maybe I should write about her photographic lineage: fourth generation, starting with her great-grandfather at the time of Daguerre, and some 60 years of professional past connecting the twenties of Berlin to the eighties of New Hampshire; or the breadth of her production: from portraits of the famed and just friends to the peopleless photograms of the fifties.

I am sure that I should write about the rediscovery of her work, starting with the Addison House monograph published in 1978, her inclusion in Margaretta Mitchell's *Recollections* (Viking, 1979), and now, the volume by Countryman Press focusing on her work of the theater and dance. It is highly personal for a viewer to state which type of work and period is most favored. I will say that the forty photographs chosen for this volume include most of my favorite Jacobi photographs.

The twenties and thirties provided Lotte with the opportunities for highly productive sessions with leading personages of the performing arts, many of them her friends. For photography, it was a period of open horizons. It was a time of experimentation, new technology and excitement over the new interaction of the arts. The photographs chosen for this volume reflect all that, and they should be treasured by us all.

A few more words about Lotte today. Living at home among her flowers, bees and birds, her days punctuated by letters to government agencies protesting their indifference to the ecology of nature and humankind, Jacobi remains a vital force, something she has been all of her life.

Cornell Capa
August, 1982

DANCE

LISELOTTE FELGER, Berlin, ca. 1930.
The shadows lined up to give the dancer a wasp waist,
adding an amusing touch to this photograph.

NIURA NORSKAYA, Berlin, ca. 1929.
Norskaya was dancing with Pavlova at the time this picture
was taken. This has become Lotte's best selling photograph.

CLAIRE BAUROFF, Berlin, 1928.
This is Lotte's second most popular photograph. She took
many pictures of Bauroff, whom she considered one of the
best and most modern dancers of her time.

CLAIRE BAUROFF, Berlin.

CLAIRE BAUROFF, Berlin.

DINAH GRACE, Berlin, 1930's.
Grace was very young when this picture was taken, but
Lotte thought she was the best dancer she ever photographed. She was amazed at how easily Grace could move
and do anything asked of her.

NONA FERY, Berlin, 1930's.
Born in Java, Fery was a talented dancer, but she was a
communist and couldn't advance professionally because of
her political beliefs.

DANCER, New York, 1940's.
Lotte saw her dancing in a theater and wanted to photograph her in costume.

MARIANNE WINKELSTERN, Berlin, 1930.
She was a popular German dancer and Lotte's neighbor.

PAULINE KONER, New York, 1939.
Lotte photographed Koner many times. She met Koner's father when she photographed the upper echelon of a Social Democratic Union; he mentioned that his daughter was a dancer. Lotte told him to send her to the studio to be photographed, and so their lifelong friendship began.

LOUIS DOUGLAS, Berlin, ca. 1932.
Douglas, an American dancer, was in a play directed by
Max Reinhardt. Reinhardt often used dancers to make his
plays more lively.

ADRIAN WETTACH ("GROCK"), Clown,
and TRUDI SCHOOP, Dancer, Berlin, 1931.
Lotte had photographed both separately but felt they
belonged together. The idea intrigued them, and they came
to her studio for a session.

HAROLD KREUTZBERG, Berlin, ca. 1930.
This well-known dancer was photographed on stage after a
performance.

PAULINE KONER, New York, 1937.
This is a montage of a photograph with a *photogenic*
(abstract photographs Lotte produced on photo paper
using direct light sources without a camera).

HANYA HOLME and Dancers, New York, ca. 1950–55.
Lotte brought only two lights to Holme's studio because she
didn't expect so many dancers. The dancers had to hold
their poses for several seconds for the proper exposure.
Hanya Holme is at the center in gray.

THEATER

ANNA MAY WONG, Berlin, 1931.
Wong was playing a dancer in a Max Reinhardt play when
this was taken. Lotte found her a likeable and fascinating
subject and photographed her on many occasions.

PETER LORRE, Berlin, ca. 1932.
Lorre was a good friend but didn't like to be photographed
in private life. When he was going to leave Berlin for Holly-
wood, Lotte asked him if she could take one picture. He
said, "Yes, one." This is it.

PETER LORRE, Berlin.
Lorre was on stage in a rare play by Karl Kraus, the most unknown and best writer in Austria in the twenties and thirties.

ACTOR, Berlin, n.d.
Lotte wanted to photograph him because of his expressive
gestures, especially the way he held a cane.

LIL DAGOVER, Berlin, ca. 1930.
Lil Dagover was Lotte's favorite actress in Berlin, and she
enjoyed being photographed by Lotte. This shows Dagover
and her dog in her car.

MICHOLS (Russian), GRANACH (German),
SISKIN (Russian), Berlin, 1929.
Granach was a close friend and brought the two
Russians to Lotte's studio. They had a lot of fun making
this photograph.

KARL VALLENTIN, Berlin, early 1930's.
A famous comedian from Munich who performed in night-clubs with Liesl Karlstadt, he also wrote some interesting books. Lotte saw him often in Munich nightclubs and asked to photograph him, but he always refused. When he came to Berlin to perform, he confessed to Lotte that he was homesick for Munich food. She offered to cook him a meal in exchange for allowing her to photograph him, and he accepted.

BRESSART and SPEELMANNS, Berlin, ca. 1929.
They were on stage in *Rivalen*.

MAX GUELSDORF, Berlin, 1920's.
He was photographed on stage at the Deutches Theater.

POISON GAS OVER BERLIN, Berlin.
The actor in the mustache played a well-known General.
The General was at the performance and laughed along
with everyone else.

THE MERCHANT OF BERLIN, Berlin, early 1930's.
The lead in this play by Walter Mehring was played by Ernst
Busch (with monocle).

GRETE MOSHEIM, Berlin, ca. 1930.
She didn't like to be photographed, but her boyfriend
wanted a picture. Lotte had to promise not to publish it,
but that was fifty years ago. This is one of Lotte's favorite
pictures.

RENÉ CLAIR, Berlin, late 1920's.
He was sent to her studio for publicity pictures for his film,
The Roofs of Paris.

HANS ALBERS, Berlin, ca. 1930.
Albers played the lead role in *The Criminals,* a very success-
ful play.

TRUDE von MOLO, Berlin, late 1920's.
She was the daughter of a famous German writer, Walter
von Molo. When she became a film actress, Lotte took the
first pictures she wanted to use professionally.

EDWARD von TWARDOWSKI, Berlin, n.d.
He is shown here playing in *The Diplomat*. Twardowski left
Berlin in the thirties for a film career in America.

ERICH WEINMANN, Berlin, late 1920's.
Weinmann is posed before a portrait of actress Lislotte
Rosen. He is dressed like a clown for a masquerade ball.

ANTON WALBROOK, Berlin, n.d.
A prominent stage actor in Germany, he moved to England, where he changed his name from Adolf Wohlbrück and became a film actor. He made many films in England and Germany, including *The Red Shoes*.

LAURITZ MELCHIOR, Berlin, n.d.
Melchior was just as good an actor in operas as he was a
singer. He is photographed with his dog and a bird Lotte
kept in her studio to entertain children.

HEINRICH GEORGE, outside Berlin, ca. 1920's.
George, a first-rate actor in Berlin in the twenties, was photographed with his child at his home.

MAGDA SCHNEIDER, Berlin, ca. 1920's.
In the twenties Lotte often went to the homes of actors to
photograph them, sessions enjoyed by both sides.

HANS RICHTER, Berlin, 1920's.
The same age as Lotte's son, he was a neighbor outside Berlin where Lotte had a summer cottage. He always wanted to be an actor, even from a very young age, and he succeeded. Last summer Lotte's son visited him, and they shared many happy memories of their youth.

EMIL JANNINGS, outside Berlin, ca. 1930.
Jannings was filming *The Blue Angel*. During a break in
shooting, he was peeling an apple, and Lotte asked if she
could photograph him. He laughed and said he didn't
mind.

KURT WEIL, Berlin, ca. 1920's.
The composer of *The Threepenny Opera,* one of the great
modern operas, he was married to Lotte Lenya at the time
this photograph was taken in his studio.

LOTTE LENYA, Berlin, 1930.
Lenya was a friend, but this was the only picture Lotte ever took of her. This remained Lenya's favorite picture of herself, and a few months before her death, she asked for prints and to be photographed again; but she died before they could get together.

93864

PN
2570
J3

JACOBI, LOTTE
THEATER & DANCE PHOTOGRAPHS.

DATE DUE
